W9-CPC-189

●═ COMMUNICATING IN A DIVERSE WORKPLACE

A Practical Guide To
Successful Workplace Communication
Techniques

Lillian A. Kuga

Richard Chang Associates, Inc.
Publications Division
Irvine, California

COMMUNICATING IN A DIVERSE WORKPLACE

A Practical Guide To Successful Workplace Communication Techniques

Lillian A. Kuga

Library of Congress Catalog Card Number
95-83811

© 1996, Richard Chang Associates, Inc.
Printed in the United States of America

All rights reserved. No part of this publication, except those pages specifically marked *"Reproducible Form,"* may be reproduced, stored in a retrieval system, or transmitted in any form or by any means, electronic, mechanical, photocopying, recording, or otherwise, without the prior written permission of the publisher.

ISBN 1-883553-69-5

Richard Chang Associates, Inc.
Publications Division
41 Corporate Park, Suite 230
Irvine, CA 92714
(800) 756-8096 • Fax (714) 756-0853

RICHARD CHANG ASSOCIATES

ACKNOWLEDGMENTS

About The Author

Lillian A. Kuga is a long standing practitioner in the Human Resources Development field. She has worked in a variety of industries ranging from electronics, aerospace and defense, to manufacturing. She is known for providing practical and successful solutions to performance development and organizational effectiveness issues. She holds a Ph.D. from Oregon State University.

The author would like to acknowledge the support of the entire team of professionals at Richard Chang Associates, Inc. for their contribution to the guidebook development process. In addition, special thanks are extended to the many client organizations who have helped to shape the practical ideas and proven methods shared in this guidebook.

Additional Credits

Editor: Ruth Stingley

Reviewer: Keith Kelly

Graphic Layout: Christina Slater

Cover Design: John Odam Design Associates

PREFACE

The 1990's have already presented individuals and organizations with some very difficult challenges to face and overcome. So who will have the advantage as we move toward the year 2000 and beyond?

The advantage will belong to those with a commitment to continuous learning. Whether on an individual basis or as an entire organization, one key ingredient to building a continuous learning environment is *The Practical Guidebook Collection* brought to you by the Publications Division of Richard Chang Associates, Inc.

After understanding the ruture *"learning needs"* expressed by our clients and other potential customers, we are pleased to publish *The Practical Guidebook Collection*. These guidebooks are designed to provide you with proven, *"real-world"* tips, tools, and techniques— on a wide range of subjects—that you can apply in the workplace and/or on a personal level immediately.

Once you've had a chance to benefit from *The Practical Guidebook Collection*, please share your feedback with us. We've included a brief *Evaluation and Feedback Form* at the end of the guidebook that you can fax to us at (714) 756-0853.

With your feedback, we can continuously improve the resources we are providing through the Publications Division of Richard Chang Associates, Inc.

Wishing you successful reading,

Richard Y. Chang
President and CEO
Richard Chang Associates, Inc.

TABLE OF CONTENTS

"I know you believe you understand what you think I think I said, but I'm not sure you realize that what you heard is not what I meant."

Anonymous

CHAPTER ONE

INTRODUCTION

Why Read This Guidebook?

The composition of today's work force is continuously evolving. Many organizations are made up of a diverse population, contributing a multitude of skills, competencies, experiences, and perspectives.

Diverse work groups within these organizations have proven to be an excellent source of new ideas and opportunities, as well as growth for each individual. Workplace diversity also creates new challenges for people who lead and manage diverse work groups. Drawing ideas from others, and effectively communicating our thoughts is tough enough when we try to communicate effectively in a diverse group, the difficulties and challenges can seem over-whelming.

This guidebook focuses on communicating successfully in diverse work groups. It contains practical tips and ideas that will help you become a better communicator in a number of everyday situations.

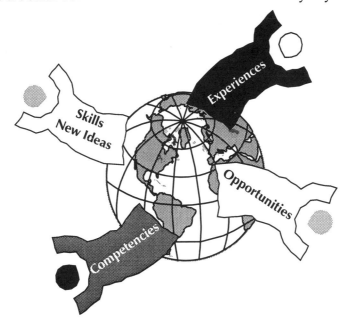

Who Should Read This Guidebook?

Anyone working with or in diverse work groups can use the tools and techniques in this guidebook as helpful resources to enhance communication skills. Readers experienced in facilitating communication will gain new ideas and approaches for improving communication in diverse work groups.

Managers, supervisors, and team and group leaders can increase their teams' effectiveness with enhanced communication and productivity. Human resources development professionals can use this guidebook as a ready reference, especially when dealing with on-going teams and cross-functional work groups. And, last but not least, this guidebook is for members of diverse work groups. As a diverse work group member, you can use it to develop your communication skills as well as to coach your peers to do the same.

When and How To Use It

Use this guidebook when you are managing or leading a diverse work group. Use it also in workshops to help managers and leaders develop their group communication skills. Incorporate the concepts when setting diverse work group norms and ground rules.

Another way to apply the concepts and tools in this guidebook is to schedule *"brown bag"* learning sessions with members of your work group. Focus on one or two of the issues that have come up in your group. Use the ideas in this guidebook to identify ways to deal more effectively with similar situations in the future.

This guidebook contains practical steps to use on the job. Planning sheets are included at the end of each chapter and reproducible forms are included in the Appendix. Copy the reproducible forms and use them in group meetings, training sessions, or in one-on-one sessions with your staff or peers.

For further reading and training application material on the topic of workplace diversity, please see the entire *Workplace Diversity Series* of guidebooks *(five titles)* of which this guidebook is part. The lead or *"parent"* guidebook in the series, *Capitalizing On Workplace Diversity*, presents an overall approach and model for an organization or work group to succeed with its diversity as one of its core strengths.

One element of this overall model, building work force capability, is expanded upon in detail in this and two other guidebooks in the series, *Successful Staffing In A Diverse Workplace*, and *Team Building For Diverse Work Groups*. Each of these guidebooks presents a platform for employees to improve the skills and competencies needed to contribute to the success of a diverse organization. The guidebooks can be used individually *(in a self-study environment)*, or they can be used in a facilitated group setting, as is the case with *Communicating In A Diverse Workplace*.

The Organizational Diversity Success Model™

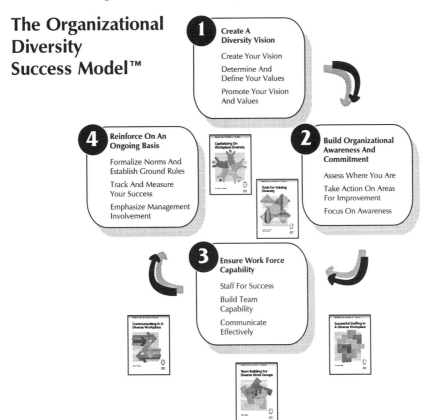

1 Create A Diversity Vision

Create Your Vision

Determine And Define Your Values

Promote Your Vision And Values

4 Reinforce On An Ongoing Basis

Formalize Norms And Establish Ground Rules

Track And Measure Your Success

Emphasize Management Involvement

2 Build Organizational Awareness And Commitment

Assess Where You Are

Take Action On Areas For Improvement

Focus On Awareness

3 Ensure Work Force Capability

Staff For Success

Build Team Capability

Communicate Effectively

THE IMPORTANCE OF COMMUNICATION IN DIVERSE WORK GROUPS

Business Communication

Advances in technology have influenced both the pace and the methods we use to communicate in an organizational setting. It is not uncommon to hear of individuals who have planned, organized, and conducted business without personally speaking to each other. Electronic mail, voice mail, faxes, and other forms of technology make this possible.

However, the apparent ease of transmitting information doesn't mean there is no longer a need for effective communication skills. In fact, some may argue that basic communication skills have become more important.

For example, a vice president of a large business-forms manufacturer personally led a series of small-group briefings with several staff members in her division to explain the company's new strategic plan. She expected to receive feedback on the plan itself, but to her surprise, most of the feedback concerned the staff's appreciation for having the opportunity to talk about things face-to-face again. The company had installed a new e-mail, voice, and on-line communication system over the last three years, and the opportunities for personal communication had taken a back seat to the new technology. She made a point of planning several more similar sessions, and encouraged the managers in the other divisions to do the same.

How do people communicate with each other in a business setting? How do we determine which mode is the most effective for a given situation? The following chart outlines some of the advantages and disadvantages of the common business-communication methods when looked at in the context of a diverse workplace.

Type Of Communication	Advantages	Disadvantages
Written communication *(including E-mail)*	◆ Exactly the same message is received by everyone. ◆ People of a different first language or those not comfortable with verbal communication often express themselves better in writing.	◆ Recipients may have different reading-skill levels. ◆ People from cultural backgrounds that value personal interaction may not take the written message as seriously as the sender intended.
Group meetings	◆ Group members have the opportunity to ask questions and seek clarification from each other. ◆ Potential communication problems can be detected or even avoided in well-facilitated meetings.	◆ Group members from certain backgrounds are less likely than others to actively communicate in group sessions.
One-on-one meetings	◆ Individuals can communicate using their own styles, without being influenced or intimidated by a group. ◆ Individuals can be more open with issues they are not comfortable with in a group setting.	◆ Some individuals may feel they are being singled out from the rest of the group. ◆ Individuals from some backgrounds are not comfortable communicating one-on-one with someone in a higher-level position. ◆ Age and gender can present challenges in one-on-one communication.
Telephone	◆ Individuals can communicate quickly and conveniently. ◆ Some of the stereotypes on style differences that present challenges in face-to-face communications are removed from the more objective style of communicating by phone.	◆ Telephone communication does not allow for non-verbal style and signals to be conveyed. ◆ People with different language abilities have a harder time communicating with someone on the phone than in a face-to-face setting.

Interpersonal Communication

The basic interpersonal communication process involves: (1) the sender formulating a message, (2) the sender encoding or sending the information to the receiver, (3) the receiver getting the message, and then (4) the receiver giving feedback to the sender that the message has been received.

TWO-WAY COMMUNICATION MODEL

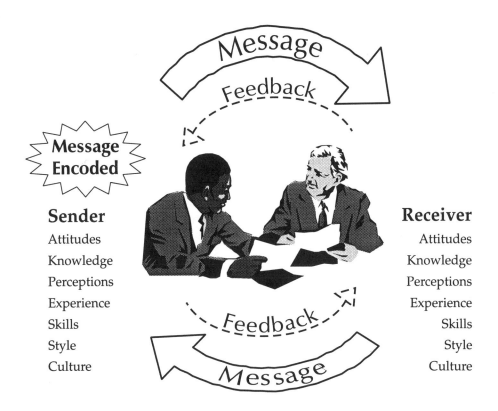

We follow this process without really thinking about the steps involved. Our communication processes, both as sender and as receiver, have been heavily influenced by many factors such as: cultural and religious background, age, gender, and first language.

Most people usually communicate best in person rather than over the telephone or in written format. In face-to-face conversation, we can see the person's facial expressions and body language that can communicate underlying factors, such as attitudes, perceptions, and style. These factors affect how messages are *"encoded"* and *"decoded."* We also pick up on other cues, such as voice inflections, and our own nonverbal behavior can enhance and punctuate the message we're trying to communicate.

Communication In Diverse Work Groups

In thinking about the topic of communication in diverse work groups, the first thing that comes to mind is the composition of the group—that is, the diversity element. Work forces today reflect diverse backgrounds, experiences, and perspectives. As we seek to define diverse work groups, our first inclination is to look at the traditional Equal Employment Opportunity (EEO) characteristics—gender, age, race, religion, and disability.

The term *"diverse"* includes consideration for the EEO factors and propels us beyond those dimensions to include a larger range of differences. Diversity implies different. Additional dimensions such as economic level, educational level, lifestyle, sexual orientation, geographical and regional differences, plus many other descriptors, are ways in which we now know diversity. It is the presence and acknowledgment of these kinds of differences in people that leads to an effective and talented work group.

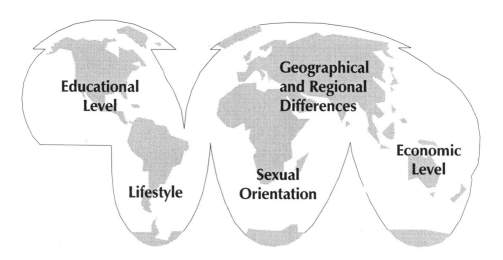

Effective communication in diverse work groups is about inclusion. It's about focusing on the effective flow of information that reaches out and captures ideas, opinions, experiences, and perspectives from people of diverse backgrounds.

Communicating in diverse work groups is a business issue. Many organizations are realizing the value of different perspectives that come with a diverse work group. Diversity can lead to more ideas and higher levels of creativity, giving the organization more options and choices, thus resulting in better outcomes for the organization and better products and services for its customers.

However, communication within a diverse work group can create complex and challenging situations. People with varying perspectives and experiences have different meanings and contexts for words and phrases. They also express nonverbals differently. What's appropriate to one person may be offensive to another.

Successful communication in diverse work groups extends beyond mastering the mechanics of basic communication and reaches into the understanding and effective use of words and phrases, knowledge about people's backgrounds, and developing positive work group relationships which foster effective communication.

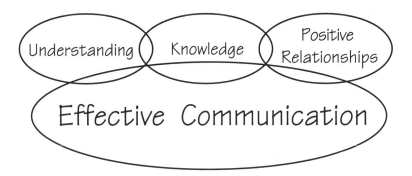

CHAPTER TWO WORKSHEET: ASSESSING YOUR GROUP'S DIVERSITY AND COMMUNICATION

1. Describe your work group by using the list below. Do the following characteristics describe your work group? Check all that apply.

My work group contains:

☐ A broad age range

☐ People of different racial backgrounds

☐ People with different religious beliefs

☐ People with disabilities

☐ People with different ethnic backgrounds

☐ People with differing educational levels

☐ People with differing economic levels

☐ People with differing lifestyles

☐ People with differing sexual orientation

☐ People from different geographical backgrounds

☐ Other differences:_____

_____

2. What kinds of communication problems or challenges have you experienced in your work group recently?

_____

_____

_____

_____

_____

_____

_____

_____

3. How do the problems or challenges listed in Question # 2 relate to your group's diversity?

_____

_____

_____

_____

_____

_____

_____

CHALLENGES AND OPPORTUNITIES

The complexity of effective communication in diverse work groups creates challenges; and, in many ways, it also provides unique opportunities for positive growth.

Marv is a manager for Ergo, Inc....

a large manufacturer of modular office furniture. The organization, in its commitment to career and management development, transferred Marv from a small regional office in a town with a population of 8,000 to an office in a large metropolitan area.

Marv is personally offended when people seem distant and aloof to his ideas. He is equally disturbed when his new staff is not receptive to brainstorming sessions. Marv feels he has strong management and organizational skills and yet, can't understand why his staff isn't responding positively to his leadership.

Marv was quite successful in communicating ideas and facilitating brainstorming sessions at his old job; however, in this new job, he is dealing with a different work force with different perspectives. In the above scenario, Marv could aggressively charge ahead. Or he could approach this as a personal and professional opportunity to increase his understanding of the new group and adapt his communication style....

Examine the following four workplace situations to better understand the unique challenges to communicating effectively in a diverse work group. You may have experienced some of these challenges yourself.

Potential Communication Challenges

Workplace situation # 1: Adding new members to the work group

◆ **When you are the new leader**
Different cultures, generations, and geographic areas have differing perspectives on the role and best style of leaders. What are the group's expectations of you as the leader?

◆ **When you're the new group member**
Work groups develop their own norms *(often informal and unwritten)* about what is and is not acceptable in the way people work together in the group—including the group's communication *"ground rules."* How will you get up to speed quickly and learn to adapt to your group?

◆ **When someone else is the new group member**
How does your work group orient new members? How does it introduce the group's diversity and communication challenges and strengths? How do new members compare their communication styles with the styles of their new group?

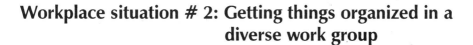
Workplace situation # 2: Getting things organized in a diverse work group

- ◆ **When influencing and motivating**
  People from various backgrounds have different responses to the motivating factors in their work environment. For example, some are motivated by recognition for individual achievements, while others place a much higher value on group accomplishments.

- ◆ **When negotiating**
  The communication styles in a negotiating setting vary widely, according to different backgrounds, gender, and so on. Some members of a work group will be comfortable with a negotiating style that other members perceive as confrontational and *"anti-team."* Other members, whose communication styles are less direct, can frustrate the more direct communicators. The direct communicators state that they can't determine where their colleagues stand on the issues.

- ◆ **Decision making**
  Decision-making approaches vary widely among people from different cultures and backgrounds. Miscommunication, and even conflict, arise when people don't understand the impact of others' perspectives, values, and expectations on group decision making. Some people, for example, are used to playing a visible role in their work group's decisions, while others have a difficult time, often because they view the group's leader as the sole decision maker.

- ◆ **Assigning responsibilities and tasks**
  All kinds of issues can make this a difficult process in a diverse work group. Differing perspectives on communication between people with different seniority levels in the organization, different ages, and different gender, all contribute to the complexity of assigning responsibilities and tasks. In addition, people from some backgrounds are open to being *"told"* what to do, while others expect a consultative process.

Workplace situation # 3: Handing ongoing work-group dynamics

♦ **Participation**
The challenge here is to avoid confusing participation with communication. Just because someone in the work group is verbal doesn't necessarily mean he is participating more, or more effectively, than someone who does not speak out as much. Work group members from different backgrounds will have different perspectives on their definition of *"participation,"* especially as it relates to communication.

♦ **Stereotyping**
We all carry our stereotypes around with us, much like the excess baggage we've accumulated over the years. Some of these stereotypes present specific communication challenges in a diverse workplace. For example, a person who has a difficult time communicating clearly in our language may be stereotyped as not having the technical skills needed for the job.

♦ **Conflicts**
Approaches to handling conflicts vary widely by culture, gender, place of geographic origin, and so on. The challenge in a diverse work group is to recognize these differences, and to ensure that initial conflicts don't escalate just because work group members have trouble recognizing and understanding each other's approach.

Workplace situation # 4: Giving and receiving feedback

♦ **Different views of feedback**
The means in which feedback is given also varies across cultures, gender, language groups, and other factors influencing us and contributing to differences. Some people are comfortable with receiving targeted feedback, while others have a very difficult time giving or receiving feedback to other members in their work group. The challenge in a diverse work group is choosing the right approach for the situation and for the people involved.

♦ **Levels of directness**
One of the most frequent communication challenges arises from differences in the level of directness in the communication process, especially in the feedback process. The issues vary—from discomfort with being singled out in *"public,"* even for positive feedback, to individual differences in the directness or indirectness of one's own feedback style.

♦ **Differences in formality**
Differences in whether feedback is presented in a formal, structured setting versus a more casual process are also a factor in diverse work groups. Some individuals expect a certain level of formality and *"protocol,"* while others operate better in a setting where feedback is more personal.

Formal

Informal

Marv decided to conduct...

an initial assessment of his situation using the overview of communication situations. He identified the critical issues as:

♦ Establishing himself as the new leader of the group

♦ Influencing and motivating the work group

♦ Encouraging participation in the work group

♦ Improving his knowledge and skill in obtaining feedback

Marv wondered if he would ever build the team he envisioned when he so enthusiastically accepted the transfer. Marv committed to turning the situation around and began focusing on his work group. He sensed communication was a problem in his new group and decided to analyze additional factors that might be contributing to the situation.

The president of Ergo, Inc. was committed to the team approach to doing business. Marv's primary responsibility in his new job was to lead a cross-functional team to streamline the procurement process. His team was formed eight months ago. Since then, the team's progress and overall productivity has been erratic due to a high turnover in team membership and ongoing group conflict.

Marv thought about what to do next as he glanced at the team roster:

- Miguel Perez
  Senior Accountant
- Sandra Stanford
  Production Manager
- Reba Washington
  HRD Manager
- Olga Petroski
  Manager Packaging Department
- Hideo Sasaki
  Purchasing Supervisor
- Anna Mae Purnell
  Senior Product Designer

Marv realized the team members had different cultural, racial, and language backgrounds and different communication styles. As a result, each person had different ideas and opinions on the best approach to this project

At the last meeting, the team discussed intra-group relations and communication. Anna Mae made a compelling presentation encouraging an off-site session. She stated, *"We need to get moving on this project and we must improve how we work with each other. I feel that on certain occasions, some of us are holding back our true opinions."*

Miguel responded, *"I don't think that's totally true. I speak my mind, and anything beyond that is no one's business. This isn't group therapy where we should spill our guts!"* Sandra shot back, *"That's not what Anna May is saying; she's talking about...."* *"Who really cares?"* interrupted Hideo. *"I mean, aren't we here to streamline the procurement process? Let's stick to the topic."* Reba chimed in with, *"Perhaps an off-site is what we need. I'm open to that idea, but we need everyone's input. By the way, when is Olga suppose to show up?"* Miguel complained, *"Now that's another thing. Olga is never here. Marv, you need to get someone who is really committed to this project. I don't think she understands how things are done in this country."* After twenty minutes of discussion, the group was far from an agreement. *"Where do I go from here?"* Marv sighed.

Communicating For Success: A Four-Step Process

There's no doubt about it; Marv is leading a diverse work group. The team members aren't listening to each other, nor appreciating the different perspectives each brings to the team.

The *Diversity Communication Planner* is a helpful tool, useful for planning and preparing *(critical for success)* for effective communication with a diverse work group.

THE DIVERSITY COMMUNICATION PLANNER

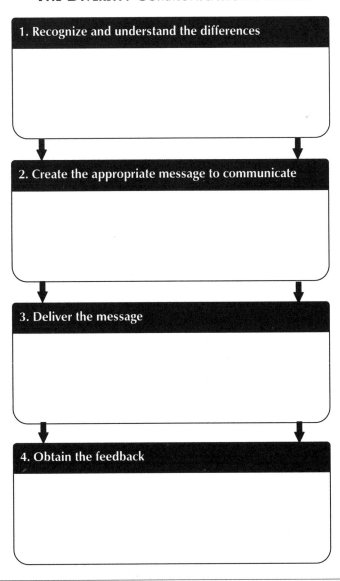

1. Recognize and understand the differences

2. Create the appropriate message to communicate

3. Deliver the message

4. Obtain the feedback

1. Recognize and understand the differences

Know who you are communicating with. What is the background of each team member? What are their experiences and how do they shape the team members' views, opinions, perspectives, and biases? Obtain a healthy insight into the work group. It's imperative to keep an open and flexible mind.

Recognizing differences means acknowledging and respecting individuals for who they are; it doesn't necessarily imply agreement with their perspectives, nor is it a like/dislike dimension.

You *(the sender)* need to consider how you are different from the intended audience. What is your background and experience, and how does the past shape your views? What are your opinions and biases? Communication is a two-way process, and you, as the sender, play an important role.

2. Create the appropriate message to communicate

Be clear about the content and goal of your message. Are you communicating to inform? Asking for input? Clarifying an issue? Resolving a problem? How should your message be formulated, given the differences between yourself and your audiences? Should your message be direct and to the point, or should it be more subtle and indirect?

3. Deliver the message

Your message can be delivered in many different ways such as written document, a team meeting, voice mail, E-mail, or face-to-face communication. Each communication mode has its own advantages and disadvantages. Select the type that will maximize the successful delivery of your message given the diversity issues involved. Knowing your audience can greatly help determine when and how to deliver the message.

4. Obtain the feedback

You will want to check for understanding and ensure that your message was accurately received. The important point is to ensure accurate comprehension, not necessarily agreement.

CHAPTER THREE WORKSHEET: ASSESSING YOUR COMMUNICATION SITUATION

1. What opportunities exist to improve or enhance communication in your work group?

_____

_____

_____

_____

_____

_____

2. Describe your work group's need for improvement. Do you need to improve feedback with the work group? Does your work group need a better understanding of how people view feedback? Or perhaps your work group needs a better understanding of people's preferences and comfort level regarding directness and formality.

_____

_____

_____

_____

_____

_____

3. What issues/challenges relating to communication in a diverse work group are you facing?

☐ Motivation, influencing *(issues/challenges):*

_____

_____

☐ Negotiating *(issues/challenges):*

_____

_____

☐ Decision-making *(issues/challenges):*

_____

_____

☐ How responsibilities and tasks are assigned *(issues/challenges):*

_____

_____

☐ Participation among the group *(issues/challenges):*

_____

_____

☐ Stereotyping *(issues/challenges):*

_____

_____

☐ Conflicts within the work group *(issues/challenges):*

_____

_____

ADDING NEW WORK-GROUP MEMBERS

When You're The New Leader

As the new leader, both you and your work group will be anticipating your first day. The work group will be wondering:

? Who is this new leader?

? What is the leadership style of our new leader?

? Will the new leader like or approve of us?

? Will we like the new leader?

The group's anticipation is further heightened by a tendency to compare you, the new leader, to the former leader. And also, you may have expectations based on work groups you have led in the past.

As the new leader it is important to be aware of the *"build-up"* that takes place by both you and the work group. You will want to determine their expectations of you as their new leader. Seek out answers to the following questions:

? What has been their communication experience (*positive and negative*) with past leaders?

? What are their preferences in communicating with the leader?

? Do they feel their own diversity is acknowledged and accepted?

The work-group members may also have expectations that are imbedded in their cultural backgrounds. Some may have assumptions and beliefs that leaders must be directive and have a strong presence whereas others are accustomed to, and expect, a collaborative, consensus-building leader. You need to find this out. Each team member's background and perspective is the starting point of how opinions of you as a leader are formed. Their assumptions influence how they will relate and communicate with you.

Learn about the members' work-related goals and objectives, as well as their professional and personal goals. What motivates them? What is important to them? What do they value? Again, personal factors such as values and motivators can influence how they communicate with you.

The following worksheet is a useful tool to help assess the situation as you start your role as the new leader.

NEW LEADER'S COMMUNICATION ASSESSMENT WORKSHEET

COLUMN I: SELF-ASSESSMENT	COLUMN II: WORK GROUP	COLUMN III: COMPARISON BETWEEN COLUMN I AND COLUMN II	
		Areas where we agree	Areas where we differ
My preferred communication style when leading work groups: ♦ ♦	The preferred communication style of the work group given its diverse make-up: ♦ ♦		
To what extent am I open and accepting of differences in others? ♦ ♦	To what extent is the work group open and accepting of differences in each other? ♦ ♦		
To what extent am I committed to full utilization of the talents and skills of each work-group member? ♦ ♦	To what extent has the work group fully utilized the talents and skills of each work-group member? ♦ ♦		
My idea of successful communication in a diverse work group is: ♦	The group's idea of successful communication within a diverse work group is: ♦		

Marv completed the Self-Assessment column...

COLUMN I: SELF-ASSESSMENT
My preferred communication style when leading work groups: ◆ Involve others, ask for their ideas and opinions ◆ Open style ◆ Collaborative approach rather than telling others what to do ◆ Give people as much information as possible ◆ Tendency to ask a lot of questions ◆ Can be directive if the situation calls for it
To what extent am I open and accepting of differences in others? ◆ I am very open to others ◆ I do get impatient with people who aren't accepting of diversity
To what extent am I committed to full utilization of the talents and skills of each work-group member? ◆ I am highly committed to fully utilizing the talents and skills of each team member ◆ We're a lean organization, and I need to have everyone working to their fullest extent on this project
My idea of successful communication in a diverse work group is: ◆ Atmosphere of openness and acceptance of ideas and opinions, where people aren't afraid to speak up ◆ Each person appreciates the contributions of everyone else ◆ Issues and problems are identified early and are resolved in a positive and efficient manner ◆ People go out of their way to keep others informed ◆ People recognize the impact of our group's diversity on communication (differing styles, approaches, and preferences, etc.)

Assessing the work group

Learn the group's history by talking with key people, such as the group members, your supervisor, and their customers *(both internal and external)*. Reviewing written communication, such as reports and meeting summaries, are also good ways to learn about the work group. Focus on the history of the group's communication successes and failures.

Look for information that will increase your ability and success as a work-group leader, in areas such as:

◆ Group dynamics (Who are the informal leaders? Followers? Who are the contributors? Do you see a pattern or style? Cliques?)

◆ Communication processes (How does information move through the work group? Passive or active forms of communication? Is language a barrier? Are people direct or indirect? How open are people to each other?)

◆ Interpersonal relationships (Who gets along with whom? Trust? Respect for individual differences? How are conflicts resolved? How long does it take for the group to get things done?)

A successful assessment requires open communication. Ask the work group for their expectations, and how they feel the group is progressing. Be accessible and demonstrate your interest in them as individuals. Your ability to foster openness depends on being trustworthy, nonthreatening, and above all, approachable. You need to convey an attitude of trust and respect. You also need to determine the extent to which diversity is truly acknowledged and respected. Is the group benefiting from the full utilization of talents and skills of each individual member?

Marv realizes he didn't consider...

all the issues related to his role as the new leader. The group had specific expectations about him. He wrote down the following notes:

This work group—

♦ Is skeptical of me as the leader as they've suffered from poor leadership

♦ Overall, prefers open and honest communication, but the recent past has made the group cautious about being open

♦ Is frustrated with their inability to effectively resolve conflict. There are a lot of differing perspectives and opinions. Everyone feels they have something to contribute; however, there seems to be a lack of appreciation for the differences in the work group.

Marv examined his expectations and realized that he came into the new job with some assumptions about leading this work group. He assumed that since the group had been together for several months, they would be a cohesive group with advanced communication skills. He realized that he needed to check his assumptions, especially in view of potential communication challenges related to the group's diverse make-up.

Marv turned to Column II of the worksheet, assessing the work group. He began by :

♦ Reviewing the group's history, looking at the meeting minutes and other such documents

♦ Spending time observing the group in different situations

   ♦ Debating issues and resolving differences

   ♦ Dealing with time pressure or deadlines

   ♦ Routine conversation

   ♦ Social conversation *(such as lunch time, or during breaks)*

♦ Scheduling and meeting individually with each group member

Marv gathered the information about the work group and recorded his observations and information on his worksheet under Column II: Work Group.

COLUMN II:
WORK GROUP

The preferred communication style of the work group given its diverse make-up:

♦ Communicate only when necessary

♦ Guarded; concerned that information revealed may hurt them

♦ Tendency to withhold information

♦ Overall sense of frustration due to miscommunication and misunderstandings

♦ Communication is strongest among close friends

To what extent is the work group open and accepting of differences in each other?

♦ Varies within the group; some are open, others have strong biases

♦ Reba and Anna Mae are very open to others

♦ Some members make derogatory comments about others' backgrounds

To what extent has the work group fully utilized the talents and skills of each work-group member?

♦ All group members have high "technical" skills, they all do their functional tasks quite well

♦ Overall, I don't think the talents of each group member is fully utilized

The work group's idea of successful communication within a diverse work group is:

♦ Information is open and readily available

♦ No surprises

♦ Proactive: "I'm informed and appraised about situations and events so I can determine how things impact my job"

♦ I get the right information to do my job correctly

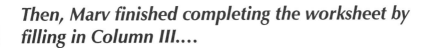
Then, Marv finished completing the worksheet by filling in Column III....

Column III:
Comparison between Column I and Column II

Areas where we agree

- Currently communication is not good; we need to improve it
- Successful communication in the group is:
  - Open, proactive
  - Information is readily available
  - A necessary tool to be successful on the job

Areas where we differ

- Each team member is at a different level regarding acceptance of diversity

- I see the value of furthering each person's contribution through better communication that will bring out existing talents not currently used. The team has been so focused on the task, they haven't realized this opportunity

- Each team member has his or her own particular style and expectation about communication. Our skill levels vary considerably

---

This assessment definitely helped Marv...

focus on communication issues. Clearly, many issues could be traced back to the diverse make-up of the group and how each person had pursued communication from his own frame of reference. He saw how acceptance and intolerance of diversity was communicated and the impact of that communication. Marv decided to build on those items which were of common interest, and prioritize areas for improving communication....

When You're The New Group Member

There may be times when you will find yourself as the new member of a work group. Perhaps someone has left the group and you have been selected as the new replacement. Or maybe the work group needs your input and expertise on an ad-hoc basis and has asked you to join them. Whatever the situation, you're coming in as a newcomer.

As the new member you'll experience some anxiety. The group will be anticipating your arrival. Both sides will be thinking about how you will *"fit"* into the group, as well as your role and responsibilities.

> ### Marv and the team realized early on...
> that the project required computer support. To streamline the work process, Banafsheh Harari, Senior Analyst from the Information Systems Division, was assigned to the team. Banafsheh was wary of the group as she had heard about some of the problems and conflicts....

Assessing the Group

As the newcomer, you're entering an existing work group that has established norms, communication patterns, and roles and responsibilities. The challenge is determining what the group's dynamics are. What is the culture? What's the personality of the work group? Participating in work-group discussions will provide insight into the group dynamics, communication patterns, and styles.

With respect to the work group, you'll need to determine its composition. Who are the individuals in the group? What differences exist? Do people acknowledge and respect these differences? What is the level of openness and acceptance of differences in others? What is the group's communication style? Is there an accepted style?

Your understanding of the group and the group's processes will help you make a positive first impression and establish your credibility. The information you gain will help you in your lead-off communication with the group members and with the group leader.

Banafsheh began her assignment...

by attending work-group meetings and interacting with the group. She noted her observations about the group's communication on the following worksheet, and felt she now had a better idea on how to approach communication with the work-group members.

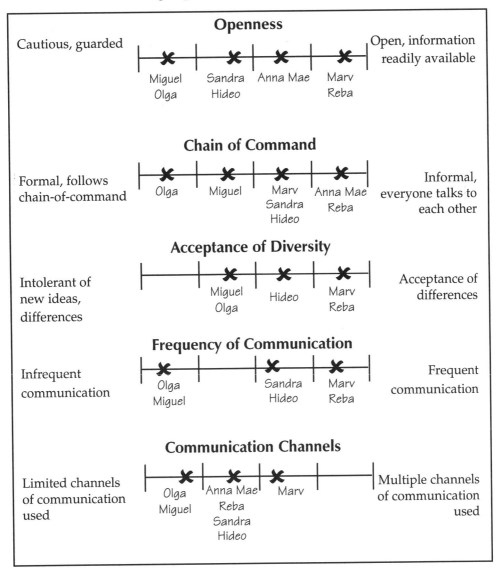

Openness

Cautious, guarded — Open, information readily available

Miguel / Olga — Sandra / Hideo — Anna Mae — Marv / Reba

Chain of Command

Formal, follows chain-of-command — Informal, everyone talks to each other

Olga — Miguel — Marv / Sandra / Hideo — Anna Mae / Reba

Acceptance of Diversity

Intolerant of new ideas, differences — Acceptance of differences

Miguel / Olga — Hideo — Marv / Reba

Frequency of Communication

Infrequent communication — Frequent communication

Olga / Miguel — Sandra / Hideo — Marv / Reba

Communication Channels

Limited channels of communication used — Multiple channels of communication used

Olga / Miguel — Anna Mae / Reba / Sandra / Hideo — Marv

When Someone Else Is the New Group Member

Put yourself in the shoes of the newcomer. Think back to a time when you were new to a group. Remember how you felt? Perhaps a little uncertain? Anxious about fitting in? Whatever your specific experience, you can count on the new group member feeling some of these jitters. As an existing member, you can and should make the newcomer feel welcome.

Get to know the new member

If the new member is coming from another part of the organization, you may already know or are familiar with the individual. However, if the member is new to the organization, the group leader typically would have some basic information on him or her, such as name, work experience, and related background. Or better yet, if the group members were actually involved in the interviewing and selection process, think of how much further ahead everyone would be in this introductory and orientation phase.

The purpose of this up-front information gathering is to learn enough about the new member to comfortably initiate conversation and establish rapport with the individual. Your preparation will enhance your ability to create a work environment of inclusion and accessibility. Remember, effective communication involves awareness building.

Facilitate the introduction of the new member

The addition of a new member can disrupt the existing balance of the group. Help other team members cope by setting the tone, and modeling openness and acceptance of the new member. Encourage the group to openly discuss communication issues, expectations, and processes, especially if there are unique considerations related to the diversity of the group.

A *"mentor program"* can be an effective way to facilitate a new member's introduction to a diverse work group. The purpose of a mentor program is to pair up a new person with an existing member. The new member knows there is someone to turn to for questions, and to help him learn and understand the organization. This type of one-on-one communication can be very effective. A mentor program can provide individualized help on issues such as:

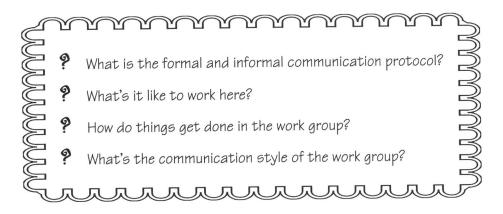

? What is the formal and informal communication protocol?

? What's it like to work here?

? How do things get done in the work group?

? What's the communication style of the work group?

The mentor can provide valuable, educational information for the new member.

Paying attention to the new member and taking a proactive position of *"what I can do to make this a good experience"* paves the way for successful communication in a diverse work group.

Marv knew in advance...

that someone from the Information Systems Division would be joining the work group, giving him time to prepare for her arrival. He used the following worksheet to create a communication plan for Banafsheh, the new member. He began by asking the work group to think of all the items a new member needed to know. He then prioritized the list using the following A, B, C code:

"A" priority: critical, needs to know immediately

"B" priority: important, items can be communicated within the next two to three weeks

"C" priority: nice to know, items can be communicated within the next three to four weeks...

"A" PRIORITY	"B" PRIORITY	"C" PRIORITY
Review with her the group's communication norms, styles, and ground rules		
Location of office • Phone number • Internal mail code	Background and history of the project	Location of office supplies
Description of the project • Deliverables, end result • Project deadline • List of work-group members and their major areas of responsibility	Meet individually with each team member to learn their roles and function	Ordering office supplies
Expectations of her roles and responsibilities • How performance will be evaluated and measured		

Marv then converted the priority worksheet into a working calendar with dates and the person responsible for communicating the items.

ITEMS TO COMMUNICATE	DATE	RESPONSIBLE PERSON
Group communication norms, style, and ground rules	October 15	Marv
Location of office	October 15	Todd, secretary
Description of project	October 15	Marv
Expectations of her roles and responsibilities	October 15	Marv
Background and history of the project	October 15	Marv
	October 19	Reba
	October 21	Hideo
Meet individually with each team member	October 25	Miguel
	October 26	Sandra
	October 27	Reba
	November 1	Olga
	November 3	Hideo
	November 4	Anna Mae
Location of office supplies	November 5	Todd
Ordering office supplies	November 5	Todd

Once the calendar was completed, Marv distributed copies to each member of the team.

CHAPTER FOUR WORKSHEET: ADDING NEW MEMBERS TO YOUR WORK GROUP

1. If you are the new leader of a diverse work group, copy and complete the New Leader's Communication Assessment Worksheet in the Appendix.

   a. Study the information in each column of the assessment you completed. Identify those areas that you feel are your work group's communication strengths.

   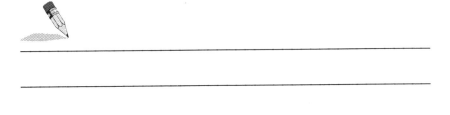

   _____

   _____

   _____

   b. What can you do to encourage these strengths?

   _____

   _____

   _____

   c. Study the information in the column labeled *"areas where we differ."* What are some opportunities for improvement? List them below:

   _____

   _____

   _____

d. As the new leader, what can you do to improve your own communication skills as they relate to successful communication in your work group?

_____

_____

_____

2. If you are a new group member:

a. Use the Diversity Communication Style continuum to assess the communication in the work group. Place an "x" on the line to indicate your assessment of the communication approaches of individuals in your work group.

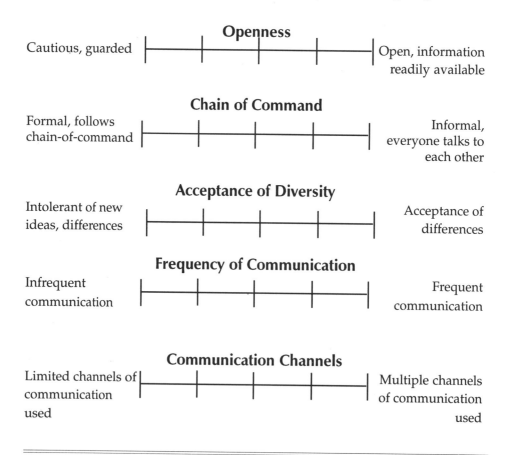

Openness

Cautious, guarded |—————|—————|—————|—————| Open, information readily available

Chain of Command

Formal, follows chain-of-command |—————|—————|—————|—————| Informal, everyone talks to each other

Acceptance of Diversity

Intolerant of new ideas, differences |—————|—————|—————|—————| Acceptance of differences

Frequency of Communication

Infrequent communication |—————|—————|—————|—————| Frequent communication

Communication Channels

Limited channels of communication used |—————|—————|—————|—————| Multiple channels of communication used

b. Analyze your observations by reviewing your assessment. As a new member entering a work group, in which areas do you think communication will be easy?

_____

_____

c. Which areas will be the most challenging?

_____

_____

d. As a new member, what can you do to facilitate effective communication?

_____

_____

3. If someone else is a new group member:

a. Will the work group be using a mentor program?

_____ yes   _____ no

If you checked "*yes*," answer the following questions.

Name of mentor:_____

Time and date of first meeting: _____

Frequency of meetings:_____

b. Use the worksheet below to create a communication plan
    for the new member. Think of all the items a new member
    needs to know, then prioritize them:

    "A" priority: critical, needs to know immediately

    "B" priority: important, items can be communicated
         within the next two to three weeks

    "C" priority: nice to know, items can be communicated
         within the next three to four weeks

"A" PRIORITY	"B" PRIORITY	"C" PRIORITY

c. Welcoming the new member

Convert the priority sheet into a working calendar or document by setting dates, times, and person responsible for communicating these items.

ITEMS TO COMMUNICATE	DATE	RESPONSIBLE PERSON

GETTING ORGANIZED IN A DIVERSE WORK GROUP

The toughest communication challenges a diverse work group faces usually come to the surface when the group is focusing on its core functions—the work it actually performs as a group. Getting work done requires organizing; planning; allocating time, money, and other resources; assigning tasks and responsibilities; and defining the roles each group member is to play. And these are not just one-time or annual events. Groups are constantly organizing and reorganizing—to deal with new challenges, to change and improve the way they work, and to accommodate changes in the group's membership *(as we saw in the last chapter)*.

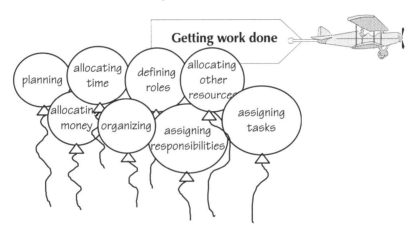

These activities involve give and take on the part of group members. Decisions will be made that might need to be *"sold"* to some of the members, since some members may be assigned responsibilities which aren't necessarily their first choices. All of the activities present opportunities for conflict and problems. What's the key to making it all happen smoothly?

Clear communication and feedback makes all the difference in the world. Since there are so many opportunities for problems to arise as a work group is organizing itself *(especially a diverse group, with different perceptions, values, and expectations)*, all group members need to be prepared to anticipate and deal with the issues.

One way to deal with these challenges is to use the Diversity Communication Planner, which was introduced in Chapter Three. It provides a methodology for people to use the communication process as a means of understanding what the real issues are, and takes into account the differences among the work-group members.

Let's look at some of the most common scenarios that present organizing challenges for diverse work groups.

◆ Assigning responsibility and tasks

◆ Influencing and motivating

◆ Negotiating

◆ Decision Making

Assigning Responsibilities And Tasks

An employee's responsibilities and tasks are typically decided early on, when the work group's planning and goal setting takes place. Strategic initiatives are translated to the working level. Answers to questions such as: *"What things need to get done?"* and *"What types of skills and competencies do we need?"* determine job scope, job tasks, and responsibilities. People are then matched to these responsibilities and tasks.

A role for both leaders and work-group members

In today's workplace, it's often possible for anyone in a work group to assign responsibilities and tasks. If the work group is operating as a self-directed work team, individual members may be responsible for giving work directions and instructions. Defining responsibilities and tasks is fairly straightforward. However, because people in diverse work groups have different perspectives and outlooks, it's important to communicate clearly on issues such as: job scope, performance expectations, and accountabilities. How these issues are communicated can make a difference in their acceptance.

Think of your own situation. What is the best way to assign work assignments? Does it depend on the assignment? What if the work is extremely difficult and risky? Or what if the work brings great rewards and is something you've been striving for? What if you're already overburdened and working twelve-hour days? For each of the scenarios listed, what would get you to accept and agree to the assignment? Your answers and reasons are as unique as each member of your work group.

In using the Diversity Communication Planner, consider asking the following key questions when your communication goal is *"assigning responsibilities and tasks."*

1. Recognize and understand the differences

♦ What do you know about this person's communication style and skills?

♦ How will the work-group member receive this task assignment? Enthusiastically? With resistance? Defensively?

♦ Will the work-group member feel comfortable in asking questions or confronting you?

♦ If not, what can you do to draw out the person and keep the communication channels open?

2. Create the appropriate message to communicate

Your message should include the following points:

♦ A description of the specific task assignment

♦ A description of why the task assignment is important to the organization and to the department

♦ WIIFM (*What's In It For Me?*)

♦ A description of the roles, responsibilities, and parameters for the assignment

♦ How long it should take to complete (*if this is a short-term assignment*)

♦ An emphasis on your support of the individual

3. Deliver the message

How will you communicate the message?
- In person?
- Written memo?
- Voice mail?
- Other:

Determine the overall tone of your delivery:
- To-the-point?
- Friendly and casual?
- Collaborative?
- Other:
- Set date and time for meeting to give task assignment
- Set location of meeting
- Make sure you've cleared your calendar so you can give full attention to your work group

4. Obtain the feedback

- Does the person understand the task assignment?
- Does the person accept the task assignment?
- Do I sense that the person will come to me with questions?

Banafsheh assessed...

the current and projected work-flow processes for the procurement project. She planned her communication to the group using the Diversity Communication Model....

THE DIVERSITY COMMUNICATION PLANNER

1. Recognize and understand the differences

- Everyone on the team will receive the task assignment.
- The task assignment is straightforward, not complicated.
- Everyone will view the task assignment as a necessary part of the project. Any concern would be around time availability; however, the team knows the information I need is critical.

2. Create the appropriate message to communicate

The specific task assignment is to submit a flow chart of current and projected processes. Since this information is available, there shouldn't be any problems. The task also includes highlighting key outputs (such as reports and recommendations).

- Their completion of this task assignment will ensure that any possibilities of automating and enhancing efficiencies will be considered.
- The work group has two weeks to complete this task assignment.

3. Deliver the message

- Ask Marv to be on the agenda for the next work-group meeting. Communicate the information that way.
- The background of a few work-group members indicate that they prefer information prior to the formal task assignment. Therefore, make sure to tell them one-on-one prior to the meeting.
- The information and task assignment is straightforward and people have seen this action item on the project schedule, so there is no need to prepare contingency plans.

4. Obtain the feedback

- Determine if anyone needs assistance or further explanation regarding the task assignment.
- Make sure I get everyone's commitment to the assignment.

Influencing And Motivating

A role for both leaders and work-group members

During the course of working together, there will be times when the work group must :

♦ Perform tasks and responsibilities of low interest (but nonetheless important)

♦ Improve or increase productivity

♦ Do things differently

When faced with these possible situations, a basic approach to assigning work may not be enough. You may find yourself selling these new or different approaches to the work group. With the movement to teams and peer-based relationships, influencing and motivating are two important skills for everyone to have.

An important starting point is understanding what motivates people. New and/or different ideas and approaches represent change, and change can be disruptive. Getting people to operate outside of their comfort zone can be difficult and challenging.

When faced with a situation where you will have to influence and motivate, refer to the following list of tips that serve as a reminder to cover important items.

TIPS FOR INFLUENCING AND MOTIVATING OTHERS

❑ Get to know each member of the work group.

❑ Examine what is important to the members of the work group. (For example, a person from a specific background may be financially motivated, while another with a different background may be driven by recognition.)

❑ Show the relevance and importance of the new idea. Explain why this is important to the organization.

❑ Point out the WIIFM. People need to see the benefit to them personally.

❑ Involve the people.

❑ Give full and complete information.

❑ Keep the communication channels open.

❑ Be accessible so people can discuss the change issue.

❑ Highlight special formats for communicating the change (such as a "hotline," bulletin-board updates, meetings, etc.).

❑ As the sender of the information, pay attention to how people are responding to your efforts at influencing and motivating. Ask yourself: "Are people interpreting my message the way I expected, given their diverse differences?"

Let's take a look at using the Diversity Communication Planner in influencing and motivating others. Following are key questions and issues to consider when planning to influence and motivate.

1. Recognize and understand the differences

♦ What do I already know about the person, especially his or her motivators?

♦ How will the person respond to the communication?

♦ What questions might this person ask, and why are those questions important?

2. Create the appropriate message to communicate

Your message should include the following points:

♦ Explanation of the situation

♦ Explanation as to why the current state is no longer acceptable or adequate *(include the need for change)*

♦ Provide the WIIFM

♦ Discussion of what specifically must change *(both the incentives and potential consequences)*

♦ Emphasize your support for the individual

♦ Address specific concerns given your assessment of the person's communication style

3. Deliver the message

How will you communicate the message?

♦ Decide the overall tone of your delivery

♦ Set date and time for communicating the message

♦ Determine the approach that the other person will be most comfortable with

4. Obtain the feedback

♦ Has the person really accepted your position?

♦ Has the person been influenced by you personally or by the rewards, consequences, or both?

Let's see how an actual discussion unfolds using the Diversity Communication Planner.

Marv just completed planning...

the weekly work-group meeting that would include a discussion of the off-site meeting. His planning and preparation took into consideration the needs and perspectives of each person. He understood the importance of recognizing the diverse background of each work-group member.

Marv began the meeting by saying, *"The first item on our agenda is the off-site meeting. We talked about it last week. There were a lot of good ideas and opinions. Today, I'd like to move forward and see if we can reach a consensus."* Marv glanced at his notes that listed his key points, and initiated a discussion of the off-site meeting:

Why is the off-site important?

♦ The work group has important issues to resolve—everyone agrees that the group isn't working well together. Ideas and opinions aren't respected, and there is much conflict and an inability to resolve it, as well as a lack of trust.

♦ These issues are holding back the progress of the project.

♦ The project directly supports an important business initiative on improving efficiency.

WIIFM

♦ Reduce or eliminate your personal frustrations with the project.

♦ Make better use of your time and effort.

♦ Successful completion of the project will be recognized by senior management.

Marv asked the group for their reaction. Anna Mae said, *"I think this is a great idea. I just want to make sure it's a productive session. I also think it's important that everyone feels comfortable with the topic; after all, we are talking about ourselves and how we aren't getting along."*

Marv couldn't help but notice that for the first time since he joined the work group, everyone was listening and nodding in agreement. *"What do you think, Hideo?"* asked Marv.

"This is the first time I heard that the project is directly tied to a larger business goal." He looked at the work-group members and added, *"We need to pull together and finish this project. But first we need to resolve our problems and put them behind us."*
As Marv gauged the group, he again noticed heads nodding and people smiling knowingly to each other.

Marv said to the group, *"Your thoughts and ideas are very important. I'm sensing that everyone agrees with the interpersonal issues in the group. Is that a correct statement?"* Everyone responded, *"yes."*...

Negotiating

The dynamic and unpredictable influences *(both internal and external)* to an organization may cause changes or adjustments to such things as work priorities, estimated schedule of tasks or project completion, planned roll-out of programs, availability of resources, the need for additional resources or information, and many other items. These work-related situations can create disagreements and conflict. Effective communication is critical.

Negotiating can be viewed as a give-and-take process that involves two or more differing perspectives. It involves examining the current situation and determining what needs to be addressed to reach a mutually acceptable solution.

Some cultures have set protocol and their own norms and procedures for negotiating, creating challenges for diverse work groups. These *"rules"* and expectations determine how a person communicates and behaves during a negotiating process.

Looking beyond cultural differences, we each have our own style that is influenced by our own comfort level and skills in negotiating. Some people find negotiating exhilarating, and approach it competitively, while others emphasize the process and prefer much debating. Still others are uncomfortable with confrontation and may back away from direct negotiation altogether.

In thinking about effective communication in the negotiation process, it's important to understand other people's perspectives:

◆ What items or things are communicated during negotiations?

◆ How are issues communicated during negotiations?

◆ Should you spend much time up front communicating "goodwill" and establishing a relationship, or should you jump in and immediately deal with the issues? This depends on the person and his/her background.

◆ Is negotiating a win-win or win-lose process? For example, in some cultures, it is extremely important to "win," and negotiating appears as a combative interaction.

◆ What is considered a successful negotiating outcome?

At one of the regularly scheduled team meetings...

in August, Marv announced to the group that he needed everyone's vacation plans for the next nine months. *"We've targeted December 18 as the day we present our recommendations for Phase I. If that goes well, then we roll out Phase II immediately. We're on a tight schedule as we must have the entire project completed by May of next year."*  Having said that, everyone all at once shouted out the days they wanted off. *"Wait, whoa,"* said Marv. *"We need to work this out as a group."* Quickly glancing at the weekly project schedule, he noticed some open time slots and said, *"Thursday afternoon is open. Can we meet at 1:00 to talk about this?"* *"Sure!"* said the team....

We will look at two different perspectives on negotiating. First, we'll look at negotiation from the leader's perspective.

A leader's perspective

A negotiation situation involving a leader and work-group members presents a unique situation. If an issue is open for negotiation, you, as the leader, must set the tone for open communication. The challenge of negotiation and communication in a diverse work group is dealing with ideas and approaches that can be quite varied and diverse. You may ask yourself, *"With a wide range of differences, will we reach a successful conclusion?"* The answer is *"yes"* if you work hard enough. Let's look at some techniques.

Work-group members may agree with the leader's position, something they normally might not do if they were negotiating with others of equal stature. Be aware of how the leader's role can affect negotiation discussions. Individuals from some cultures and backgrounds may be uncomfortable negotiating in any way with someone in a senior position. Establish guidelines for discussion to encourage people to contribute.

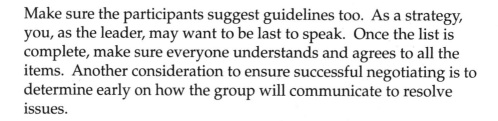

♦   Everyone has equal input

♦   Everyone contributes

♦   Stay focused on the topic

♦   Decisions and conclusions will be reached by consensus

♦   All ideas and suggestions will be acknowledged

Make sure the participants suggest guidelines too. As a strategy, you, as the leader, may want to be last to speak. Once the list is complete, make sure everyone understands and agrees to all the items. Another consideration to ensure successful negotiating is to determine early on how the group will communicate to resolve issues.

> ♦ Who decides what is *"open for negotiation?"*
>
> ♦ What will be the group process regarding negotiating issues?
>
> ♦ What happens if communication gets bogged down?
>
> ♦ What happens if the parties involved reach an impasse?

Anticipate questions and potential problems; then work those items into an action plan. Make sure that everyone understands and agrees to the negotiating norms, and ensure that the norms are communicated.

A work-group member's perspective

Negotiating is a skill. When working with others who are less-skilled negotiators, the negotiating process may take longer. Consider training group members in this area if you feel they need improvement.

Once again, let's see how the Diversity Communication Planner can be used in this type of scenario.

1. Recognize and understand the differences

How will the work-group member react to negotiations?

♦ Enthusiastically?

♦ With resistance?

♦ Defensively?

Will the work-group member feel comfortable in asking questions or confronting me? If not, what can I do to draw out the person and keep communication open?

2. Create the appropriate message to communicate

The following list will help you get started in your initial communication. Keep in mind that negotiation can be a lengthy process. You may or may not reach a conclusion after one round of discussion.

Your message should include the following points:

- The need for, and importance of openly discussing *(that is, negotiating)* the issue

- The issue at hand, including the different points of view

- An expression of your willingness to listen and to consider other points of view

- A discussion of each person's expectations regarding the negotiation discussion. That is, what do you and the other person hope to obtain from the discussion?

- A discussion of time deadlines and other resource constraints *(if applicable)*

3. Deliver the message

- How will you begin negotiating?

- Determine the overall tone of your delivery

- Set date and time for initial meeting

- Set location of meeting

4. Obtain the feedback

You will want to get feedback on the following:

- Do each of you understand the key points and elements of the negotiation issue?

- Do each of you understand the other person's point of view? *(You don't necessarily have to agree, just understand.)*

- Do each of you feel that your thoughts and opinions are acknowledged and respected?

Reba offered a suggestion...

on scheduling vacations for the work group. She said, "*Why don't we tape up nine flip-chart sheets and label them September through May? Then we can list who wants to take time off each month. That way we can see if there is a conflict with the project schedule as well as each other's vacation plans.*"

Everyone, except Olga, nodded in agreement with Reba's idea. Reba noticed Olga's lack of response and said, "*Before we tape up the flip-chart sheets, I want to make sure everyone thinks this is the right thing to do. I don't want you to feel I'm forcing this idea on you.*" Hideo replied, "*Believe me, Olga, if I felt you were forcing us to do this, I'd say something!*" "*Yep, we sure would,*" said Anna Mae. This caused a lot of laughter in the group. But Olga wasn't laughing.

"*Just to make sure, let's quickly go around the room and check,*" said Reba. Reba proceeded to ask for each team member's opinion. Each person responded positively until she came to Olga. Olga replied, "*I guess this is okay. It's just so different to have workers decide on the vacation schedule. I'm used to the boss approving or denying vacation requests, and no questions asked. Where I come from, that's the way things were. But I'm beginning to understand your ways of doing things. It's just so different.*"

"*You know, Olga, this is new to all of us,*" reassured Miguel. Everyone nodded and smiled at Olga. She immediately felt more comfortable. "*If it will help, let's take our time, within reason, in hashing out this vacation issue,*" suggested Banafsheh. "*Marv, when do you absolutely need this information? We may need several days to come up with a schedule. Besides, I think it's important that we're all comfortable with the negotiating process, and that the process works for us.*"

The group members zeroed in on Olga's discomfort with negotiating vacation time. They had been working with Olga long enough to realize that her background was a big factor in affecting her initial attitude and opinion of the group determining the vacation schedule. Olga made strides in accepting the differences in her team. She no longer shut down conversation, but kept the communication door open. With regards to negotiating vacation plans, the rest of the work group was willing to take a slower pace and help Olga....

Decision Making

A role for both leaders and work-group members

In some organizations, the leader is responsible for ensuring that effective decision-making takes place in the work group. For a self-directed work group, most decision making is a shared responsibility. Communication is the key element that supports effective decision making.

If you are designated and accountable for decision-making outcomes, use the following checklist to plan and proceed:

☐ Have you communicated clearly so everyone understands the decision and its implications?

☐ Does your work group know its role in decision making?

○ Is it to make a recommendation only?

○ Is it to share decision making with the leader?

○ Is it full accountability and responsibility for decision making?

The goal is to approach decision making with clear, concise communication and to prevent any misunderstanding of the basic issues surrounding the decision.

Effective decision making assumes that the people involved have decision-making skills and understand the decision-making process. It is worth the time and investment to assess the decision-making skills of group members, and provide training if needed.

1. Recognize and understand the differences

- Who will be involved in the decision-making process?

- What do you already know about them?

- Will the work-group member(s) feel comfortable in contributing ideas and asking questions?

- If not, what can you do to draw them out and keep the communication open?

2. Create an appropriate message to communicate

Your message should include the following points:

- A description of the decision which must be made

- An explanation of why the individual is involved in the decision-making process

- WIIFM

- An identification of the roles and responsibilities involved in the decision-making process

3. Deliver the message

The following information focuses on when you are actually involved in the decision-making process.

- How will your thoughts and views be communicated during the decision-making process?

Determine the overall tone of your communication during the decision-making process. Will it be:

- To-the-point?
- Collaborative?
- Friendly and casual?

4. Obtain the feedback

You need to get feedback on the following:

♦ Do each of you feel there was open communication?

♦ Did you come across as being objective?

♦ Did your thoughts and ideas come across as you intended?

♦ Do you understand the thoughts and ideas of the other person?

♦ Do each of you feel that differences of opinions and ideas were respected?

♦ Do each of you feel as satisfied as possible with the outcome?

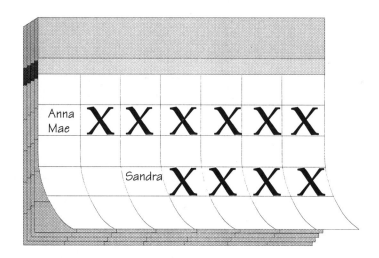

The work group was in the midst...

of determining the vacation schedule. Marv was pleased with the interaction and communication, especially in how each member paid attention to the background and differences of others. He was interested in speeding up the process and was ready to suggest a task team to finalize the schedule.

He thought about how this decision process would be communicated to the group.

1. Recognize and understand the differences

♦ Each work-group member has his or her own unique communication style, and the communication skills have greatly improved.

♦ Given my understanding of all team members as well as their capabilities, I think I'll ask for volunteers for the task team instead of appointing them. This way, the group will be making the decision and not me.

♦ A couple of the individuals are still not comfortable with communicating their individual positions if they sense it is different from the group.

2. Create the appropriate message to communicate

♦ The purpose of the decision is to determine who will serve on the task team.

♦ The role of the task team is to complete the vacation schedule, with input and review from the entire group.

♦ Reassure the group that the task team must review the schedule with them before final approval. This should ease their concerns and therefore cover the WIIFM.

♦ The task team has three days to complete their assignment.

3. Deliver the message

♦ Timing is good in that our next meeting is tomorrow. I'll cover the information then.

♦ Since this is a group-based decision, I need everyone together in one room.

4. Obtain the feedback

♦ I'll know if I'm coming across clearly by the questions they ask.

♦ Since my goal is for the group to make a decision, I'll view the decision as a criterion for determining successful communication.

CHAPTER FIVE WORKSHEET: GETTING ORGANIZED IN YOUR DIVERSE WORK GROUP

1. Is your work group getting bogged down in its work process? Are you at a loss as to where to begin? The following exercise can help you identify areas to focus on. Place a check mark by the items that describe your situation.

Assigning Responsibilities and Tasks

☐ Members are bored with their job

☐ The department is growing and taking on new responsibilities and tasks

☐ We need to expand and broaden the skills of existing members

☐ Members are asked to serve on special projects in other areas of the organization

Influencing and Motivating

☐ Work-group members must improve and/or increase productivity

☐ Work-group members must perform job task/functions differently

☐ Work-group members must perform tasks and responsibilities of low interest

☐ Work-group members must perform new responsibilities

Negotiating

- ☐ Work-group members cannot effectively resolve conflict

- ☐ Work-group members must compete for resources

- ☐ Work-group members get defensive when trying to resolve differences

- ☐ Work-group members become argumentative when trying to resolve differences

Decision Making

- ☐ A single work-group member dominates group decision making

- ☐ The work group makes poor decisions

- ☐ The work group spends too much time reaching a decision and/or reaching a conclusion

- ☐ The work-group members do not understand their roles when asked to participate in decision-making meetings

2. Review your results. Which of the items checked are related to the communication issue in your work group? What role does the group's diversity play?

_____

_____

_____

_____

_____

_____

COPING WITH ONGOING DYNAMICS IN A DIVERSE WORK GROUP

Participation In Groups

What makes some people *"better"* participants in work groups than others? Why do some people actively participate while others hold back? The answers to these and other related questions depend on whom you ask. Your own personal expectations and definition of *"active participation"* may be different from others in the work group.

If you are used to high interaction and a lot of discussion, a passive, quiet individual will appear to you as a non-contributor. Some people may appear hesitant to you, but to themselves, they are behaving normally. The level of communication and participation in a diverse work group is influenced by each person's background, opinion, and cultural perspective. Therefore, if you are asked to facilitate or be a part of a group, an up-front assessment of how people define and view participation is important.

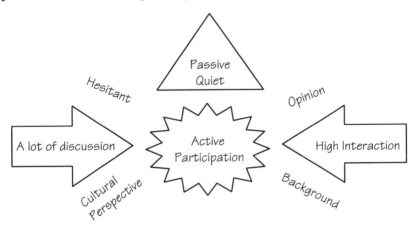

Olga Petroski, Manager of the Packaging Department...

has worked for Ergo, Inc. for thirteen years. The team concept was new to her, and the adjustment had been difficult. Olga firmly believes in doing her work well and keeping socialization to a minimum. During team meetings, Olga thought to herself, *"Why should I spend time chit-chatting when I could be doing my job? This is not how work should be done."* Olga often skipped meetings because she felt they interrupt her work schedule.

Anna Mae thinks and talks at the same time. She moves quickly from idea to idea and others have a difficult time following her. But it all makes sense to Anna Mae. Highly-interactive and lively team meetings are stimulating to her. She thrives on emotional expression. Olga and Anna Mae are members of the same diverse work group and have problems communicating with each other....

These examples are not unique. There are a multitude of reasons why participating and communicating in work groups can be difficult. What are some of the issues related to a group's diverse make-up? Let's take a look:

- ♦ **Cultural background.** This can either encourage or discourage free-flowing expression.

- ♦ **How members view the team leader.** How do members from different backgrounds view their relationships with someone in a leadership role?

- ♦ **Different ways in which members process information.** Some people need time to think and analyze a key point before responding. Does this mean they're dull and non-participatory? No, it means they're processing and assimilating the information. On the other hand, some people are spontaneous and will react immediately to what is said.

- ♦ **Language proficiency.** Think of how you might feel if you are in a meeting where the discussion was in a language you didn't know well. It would be very difficult to participate. Language proficiency does influence participation.

What can you do to encourage healthy participation in diverse work groups?

♦ Stay focused on the goal. Participation that is focused is appropriate, follows the topic or agenda, and adds meaning and value to the discussion. It's not necessarily how long or how little a person talks. You are looking for a richness of discussion that comes from tapping into the background and experience of the diverse work group.

♦ Identify each member's needs and requirements for comfortable participation. You may want to conduct a group exercise in which each member lists a necessary condition that must exist in order for him or her to participate in the group. Two examples are: "Everyone listens objectively before responding," and "No personal attacks or criticism."

♦ Acknowledge and reward participation by thanking people for their input; and, whenever possible, use their ideas.

♦ Make sure that group discussion is well facilitated and monitored. Don't let the discussion degrade; keep it on track and balanced.

♦ Sponsor a training program on group participation. People may lack the understanding, knowledge, and skills of effective group participation.

Marv was at his desk reviewing the agenda...

for the upcoming team meeting. Pleased with the team's progress, he said to himself, *"Yes, we've struggled, but we've made a lot of progress. Now, for this brainstorming session, I really want people to feel their time has been well spent."* Marv checked his notes. He thought to himself, *"Everyone knows my style and that I've been straight with them—when I say we're going to brainstorm, they know that their input counts. Even Olga is getting more involved in these open brainstorming sessions. Everyone understands the problem—procurement data and information mysteriously have fallen out of the system."*

Marv knew it was a sensitive topic, as the group had worked long hours on the data inputting and reporting modules. He couldn't afford to have the group lose focus now. He needed the group to stick to the issue and stay away from personalities. He also needed to have full participation and was concerned that some group members might *"hold back."*

There are essentially two approaches you can take to encourage participation. Each has its own implications for the communication process between yourself and other members of the work group:

☑ **The personal approach.** This involves seeking and getting participation based on relationships, personal appeal, and your skills in the areas of communicating and influencing.

☑ **The joint-task approach.** This approach emphasizes the specific involvement each member will play in a given task or project, and does so in such a way that members play a role in defining their participation. In other words, there is more joint planning than "selling" to encourage participation.

Both of these approaches assume, of course, that the group members view the roles and tasks in which they are being asked to participate as meaningful and relevant. If people are resisting or asking *"Why should I be doing this?"* you need to go back to the WIIFM first. Only then can you really focus on high-quality participation.

In reality, we all use both approaches in combination. The key is to know when to shift emphasis back and forth to fit the situation and the make-up of the group itself. Let's look at an example in which the emphasis is on the joint-task approach.

Marv facilitated the group brainstorming session...

and had them analyze the problem. The group gradually narrowed their list to three possible causes of the problem and recorded them in the first row.

He then opened up the discussion to look at underlying *"root"* causes. Marv used the *Communication-Problem Analysis Chart* to help the group with the next step, peeling back the layers of each cause to understand what's behind it....

COMMUNICATION-PROBLEM ANALYSIS CHART

	Cause #1 *Errors in inputting data* **Why?**	Cause #2 *Problem with computer program* **Why?**	Cause #3 *Hardware problems* **Why?**
1.	**because...** *working too fast, keystroke errors* **Why?**	**because...** *problems in downloading files* **Why?**	**because...** *system overloaded* **Why?**
2.	**because...** *untrained* **Why?**	**because...** *error in code* **Why?**	**because...** *breakdown in linkages* **Why?**
3.	**because...** *some out-of-date equipment* **Why?**	**because...** *hasn't been updated in more than a year* **Why?**	**because...** *some out-of-date equip-ment* **Why?**

The group then brainstormed...

possible solutions and agreed on three different criteria to assess the solutions. The group evaluated each possible solution against the criteria. They used a scale of 1-10, where 10 is the highest....

	Solution 1	Solution 2	Solution 3	Solution 4
	Train Data Entry	Establish quality check points	Audit programming codes	Consult with vendors regarding hardware
Criterion A *Cost* *10=most cost-effective*	5	9	5	8
Criterion B *Highest probability of solving the problem=10*	5	4	10	2
Criterion C *Time* *10=quickest to get done*	4	5	6	5
Total Score	14	18	21	15

The group then completed a plan of action using the following worksheet.

Action Step Task/Activity	Responsible Person/Group	Completion Date
1. Identify key people to conduct audits	Banafsheh, Marv	October 1
2. Meet with auditing group and determine course of action	Banafsheh, task team leader	October 4
3. Determine which codes to audit	Banafsheh, with input from audit team	October 6
4. Conduct audit	Audit team	October 28
5. Report on results of audit	Audit team	October 31
6. Determine next steps (e.g. rewrite codes)	Audit team	November 3

Now let's take a look at how the stereotypes we hold can effect communication in a work group.

Stereotyping

Stereotyping can hurt both productivity and the sense of team spirit. The presence of diversity in a work group may increase the chances of stereotyping. Let's look at how stereotyping can hurt a group.

Miguel was not pleased with Olga's behavior...

in the work group. In Miguel's opinion, she missed a lot of meetings, and when she did attend, she didn't participate. Miguel quickly grew impatient and immediately began associating the negative behaviors with Olga's ethnic background.

At the end of one long, exhausting work session with the work group, Miguel commented as he was packing his briefcase, *"I hope I never have to work with her again!"* He was referring to Olga. *"People from that region are not team-oriented, prefer to work alone, and don't appreciate our humor,"* he said.

Reba, the HRD Manager responded, *"I think Olga has given us good ideas. Yes, she's quiet, but don't hold that against her. I'm quiet too, sometimes."* Miguel shot back, *"That's the problem with you women!"*

Reba's eyes flared with anger and she was about to respond when Marv walked in. *"Oh, I thought everyone had left. I just need to collect the flip charts,"* said Marv. Marv had caught the last part of the conversation and was disturbed by Miguel's remarks. Marv turned to both of them and remarked, *"It's been a long day and I know we're all exhausted. We did get a lot done today."* He paused and said, *"But is there something going on that I should know about?"*

Miguel replied, *"Yes, the entire process would move faster if we worked together as a team. We really do need people committed to the project and I don't think everyone is."* Marv replied, *"I'm aware of the frustrations this group is experiencing and I'm committed to getting us through this. Miguel, can you stop by my office first thing tomorrow morning?"* *"Oh, sure,"* said Miguel, puzzled as to why Marv wanted to talk to him....

Miguel's comments about Olga and about women are examples of negative stereotyping. Negative stereotyping arises when negative impressions and opinions are turned into broad generalizations and projected onto a specific group or classification of people. The bad feelings Miguel had toward Olga could cross over into daily communication and impact their working relationship on the project.

What do you do when you see or hear stereotyping in your work group? One approach is to meet with the offender and deal with the issue immediately.

Miguel peered into Marv's office...

and said, *"You wanted to see me?"* *"Yes, Miguel, please come in. Have a seat,"* Marv responded, offering him a chair. *"Miguel, when I walked into the conference room last night, I couldn't help but overhear some remarks you made about Olga. You sounded pretty frustrated and angry. I'm concerned about your view of Olga. Why don't we talk about it?"* suggested Marv....

Marv had to talk to Miguel about stereotyping. What did Marv say to Miguel? What did he address? Here's what he did and also what you can do if you are in a similar situation.

♦ Confront the issue. Let the offender know that what was said or done is stereotyping, and it is not tolerated. This includes verbal and written comments. Jokes that highlight stereotypes should be confronted and dealt with.

♦ Explain to the offender what you do want to see and hear. Emphasize the importance of individual skills and competencies; stay away from making personality judgments and generalizations.

♦ Explain and reinforce the importance and value of diversity in a work group.

♦ Make sure the person understands the seriousness of the situation.

♦ Get a commitment from the person that he will do his best to avoid negative stereotyping in the future.

Positive stereotyping is equally as damaging. Why? Even though the stereotype may focus on positive qualities, it still limits one's full vision and scope of the individual. You see the person only in a limited capacity. This type of stereotyping can influence thinking and *"box in"* a work-group member to a few, specific tasks. It limits the member's growth and causes frustration.

Managing Conflicts

Conflicts seem inevitable in groups, especially diverse work groups. Conflicts can arise for a number of reasons:

- ◆ Miscommunication due to language or communication-style differences

- ◆ Differing personal-interaction styles relating to diverse backgrounds

- ◆ Work pressure

- ◆ Being irritated by an individual's mannerisms which may be very different from what is the norm in another individual's culture

Communication during conflict in a diverse work group is extremely challenging, because:

- ◎ Emotions are charged
- ◎ There's a tendency to display behavior typically not used during normal circumstances
- ◎ Each culture has its own way of expressing and dealing with conflict

Marv's work group met to discuss...

preliminary recommendations for streamlining the procurement process. The group went through the first three agenda items smoothly. However, the fourth item caused some argument. *"The purchasing standards you're recommending will result in packaging material that will not protect the furniture during shipment,"* said Olga.

"But Olga," said Hideo, *"the purchasing standards will let us go with one vendor. We'll have one source to work with which means we don't have to do competitive bids. We'll save time and money. Can we change the packing materials or even look at alternative forms of shipment?"*

"This is not my area," said Anna Mae. *"I can't redesign the furniture for greater durability during shipment." "Don't get defensive,"* responded Hideo. *"I'm not!"* said Anna Mae. Sandra Stanford, the Production Manager, offered, *"Maybe we should revisit the purchasing standards."*

The group was in conflict. How could Marv bring the discussion back on course?

The following steps can help when your work group is in conflict.

♦ Decide if it's okay to proceed, or if the group needs a temporary break. If emotions are highly charged and the group members have temporarily lost their ability to be objective, you may want to table the issue and revisit it at a later date.

♦ Establish or revisit the guidelines for group discussion.

♦ Define the issue or problem objectively.

♦ Agree on the end result; that is, ask the group what it is trying to achieve.

♦ Get everyone's commitment to working on a successful resolution.

♦ Make sure there is a facilitator who can keep the discussion on track, and communication channels open.

CHAPTER SIX WORKSHEET:
COPING WITH ONGOING DYNAMICS IN YOUR DIVERSE WORK GROUP

1. As you think about ongoing dynamics, what are some of the specific challenges in your diverse work group?

    a. Participation

    _____

    _____

    _____

    _____

    b. Stereotyping

    _____

    _____

    _____

    _____

    c. Conflicts

    _____

    _____

    _____

    _____

2. Write the problem statement for each situation you've identified in clear and concise terms.

a. Participation

_____

_____

_____

_____

_____

b. Stereotyping

_____

_____

_____

_____

_____

c. Conflicts

_____

_____

_____

_____

_____

3. Describe the *"desired state"* you hope the group can reach for each situation.

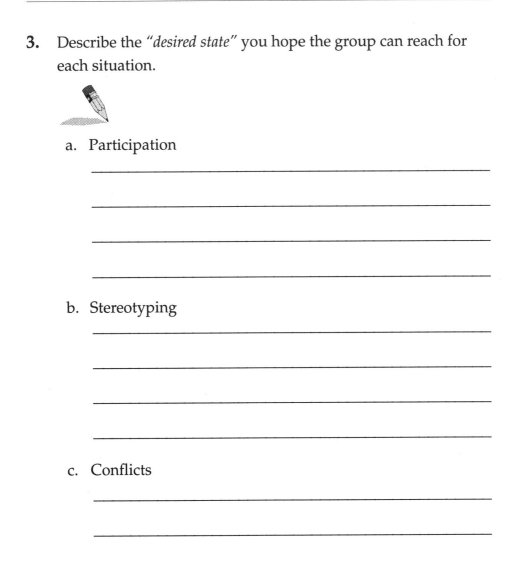

a. Participation

_____

_____

_____

_____

b. Stereotyping

_____

_____

_____

_____

c. Conflicts

_____

_____

_____

_____

4. Select one of the problems described above. Use the blank Communication-Problem Analysis Chart, the Criteria Rating Form, and the Action Planner in the Appendix to address these selected communication problems in your next group meeting.

GIVING AND RECEIVING FEEDBACK IN DIVERSE WORK GROUPS

Routine, day-to-day communication is challenging in and of itself. Communicating feedback is more difficult, and yet it is very important because effective communication includes feedback. Feedback is an indication of how well your message is accurately sent and received. That is you discover if your message is being received in the way you intended. The goal of feedback is to get confirmation of your message.

Giving and receiving good feedback depends on following effective communication practices and approaches in diverse work groups.

- ◆ Understand the members of your work group
- ◆ Learn different communication approaches and strategies
- ◆ Use good communication techniques effectively and judiciously

These practices will increase your chances of giving and receiving effective feedback.

Some cultures discourage feedback, especially from a subordinate to a superior. Age can also be an issue if a younger person is having to give feedback to someone older. Communication styles also impact feedback. For example, an individual with a background of communicating facts may have difficulty in communicating feelings as a form of feedback.

Two Different Views Of Feedback

When someone mentions feedback, what is the first thing you think of? Perhaps it's a recent incident, such as performance-appraisal feedback from your supervisor, or feedback on a presentation you did. What feelings or emotions do you associate with feedback? Do you enjoy giving feedback? How about receiving feedback? Many people will say how important feedback is, and at the same time will agree that it's a difficult process to handle effectively and comfortably.

Traditional—or top-down—feedback

The traditional feedback format consists of someone in a higher or superior position giving feedback to someone of lower rank or level; hence the name *"top-down."* The responsibility lies with the sender to effectively communicate the message to the receiver. The receiver plays a passive role in this feedback process. The individual listens to and/or reads the comments, then gives feedback.

Consider the traditional form of feedback in a diverse work group. If the supervisor is responsible for giving feedback to the work-group members, the feedback is obviously coming from only one source. Think of how much information and learning is missed by not getting feedback from others who may have valuable input because of their different perspectives.

The task of giving good feedback becomes more challenging and is heightened by the diversity factor. Some people may prefer the traditional format and are comfortable with top-down feedback. Others may be frustrated by the format and want a more interactive discussion as it relates to the entire communication and feedback process. Let's take a look at some key considerations regarding the traditional format.

♦ What is your skill level and comfort level in giving feedback in a traditional, top-down approach?

♦ What modes of communication will you use (for example, face-to-face, e-mail, voice mail, or written communication)? Can you effectively give feedback through these different modes?

♦ Does the work situation give you an opportunity to accurately observe and assess each work-group member?

♦ Do you have time to pull together feedback for each work-group member?

♦ Are you able to consider the unique differences of each work-group member as you prepare the feedback; that is, can you take into consideration the diversity element?

♦ Are all members of your diverse work group open and comfortable with the traditional format?

♦ Will the traditional format give you and the diverse work-group members the type of feedback necessary to monitor performance and progress? Is it appropriate?

Marv prepared formal performance appraisals...

according to the organization's policy. Although the format suggested a traditional form of feedback, Marv knew he could make the communication collaborative and an open discussion. Marv was comfortable with the entire range of giving feedback. He looked at the list of work-group members and said to himself, *"I need to make this communication comfortable for each of them. If I approach it from their comfort level, perhaps the feedback will have a greater impact."*...

Marv was on target in assessing the formal performance appraisal and paying attention to the differences in each of his work group members. He made the following notes:

PERSON	FEEDBACK
Miguel	Tone of delivery should resemble a traditional, top-down approach. Leave room for Miguel's comments, as he has a need to comment back.
Banafsheh Sandra Reba Hideo Anna Mae	Make sure all feedback comments are on the form and use the form more as a "discussion guide." Tone of delivery should be highly collaborative. Leave lots of room for comments. Anticipate them giving me feedback as well.
Olga	Tone of delivery should resemble a traditional, top-down approach. Need to encourage Olga to give comments.

Multi-source feedback

Multi-source feedback means that feedback comes to an individual from a variety of sources—such as the supervisor, peers, subordinates, and customers. Multi-source feedback is commonly referred to as multi-rater, 360 degree feedback, and peer feedback. This format is increasingly being used with self-directed work groups who share management-type tasks and accountabilities. In fact, the accountability for performance in a work group is to each other.

How might the multi-source format work in a diverse work group? Some members might readily endorse and want to have this type of feedback. Others may be uncomfortable in evaluating their peers as well as get feedback from sources outside the work group. In a diverse work group, you know that opinions and comfort level will vary.

The work group was finishing the final phase...

of the project. Marv received a packet of information from Human Resources asking for a final evaluation of the project. The evaluation specifically focused on the group and asked for feedback from internal and external customers. In addition to this, the work group gave feedback to their internal and external sources.

Marv shared the packet with the work group. The response from Sandra, Reba, Hideo, and Anna Mae was summed up by Anna Mae's comment, *"I think this is terrific. I like knowing how I'm doing, because sometimes it's difficult for me to figure out. I'm so glad this is a two-way street. I'm looking forward to giving feedback to the other departments that we depended on!"*

Olga had developed and modified her communication skills throughout the project, especially those related to communicating with people who were different than her. She, however, was the most hesitant with multi-source feedback. She was brought up in a culture that had led her to firmly believe that employees take orders, do the work, and wait to hear from their superiors about their performance. Multi-source feedback was a new concept to her. But she said, *"We've come this far, and the project is almost over. I'm willing to try this multi-source feedback, or whatever you call it. Just tell me how it works."*...

Multi-source feedback can be more spontaneous, because the sender often receives immediate feedback on how well the message is coming across. It also gives people feedback from others *(customers)* who are the recipients of their service or product and are therefore impacted by their performance. Let's take a look at some key considerations for using multi-source feedback.

Specifically, what type of feedback format will be used?

♦ A peer-group session where all members of the work group give verbal feedback to each other?
    -or-
♦ A written assessment where the results are tabulated and given to the individual?

How and when will the leader give feedback? The following list contains helpful ideas and techniques for putting in place an effective feedback process for a diverse work group.

♦ How will the work group take into consideration the unique differences of each member as they prepare feedback?

♦ Are all members of the diverse work group open and comfortable with the multi-source format?

♦ Will the multi-source format give you and the diverse work group members the type of feedback necessary to monitor performance and progress? Is it appropriate for the situation?

♦ Are the work-group members skilled and comfortable in giving and receiving feedback?

♦ Does the work situation give each member an opportunity to accurately observe and assess the work of his/her peers?

If possible, select diverse work-group members who support and buy into the format.

For example, XYZ corporation decided to open a satellite office that would operate as a self-directed work organization. Since this was a new operation, the company needed to hire new employees. One of the hiring criteria was openness and comfort in working in a self-directed work environment. Management had already determined that the operation would use a multi-source feedback format. This was also a key factor in the hiring process.

Once the employees were hired, management explained the multi-source format structure and gave them the context of feedback. Management gave employees the opportunity to determine the spontaneity and frequency of giving feedback, and what issues and topics would be open and communicated. Feedback was expanded to include job performance. The team members had input on the order and type of skills and competencies that would be evaluated. As they gained confidence in giving formal peer feedback, receivers were allowed to formally and objectively give feedback to the senders.

- If necessary, train the work group on feedback skills, both giving and receiving feedback.

- Make sure the work group has available to them a skilled coach or facilitator.

- Coach the work-group members on their feedback delivery.

- Identify specific needs of the work-group members; and, if necessary, work with them on an individual basis. For example, does it seem that strong cultural beliefs are working against the feedback format? Keep in mind you are not trying to change or replace cultural beliefs. You want the work group to adjust and settle into a comfortable practice of communication and feedback.

- The focus is on helping work-group members build skills so they can communicate feedback appropriately to their peers.

- Give positive reinforcement for on-target behavior.

Levels Of Directness

Directness is an important element of diverse work-group feedback and communication. Regardless of the feedback format or structure (*traditional or multi-source*), the diverse work-group members will have their own comfort levels and preferences in how direct and straightforward they want to be in giving feedback.

What is the impact of directness on feedback? Consider the following example.

Hideo reviewed a presentation...

by Sandra on production capacity. At the end of the presentation, Hideo said matter-of-factly, *"The information is hard to follow, your second overhead has a typo, and you need to project your voice."* Sandra was stunned by Hideo's remarks and was not sure how to respond. *"Yes, this is feedback,"* she thought to herself, *"and the purpose of Hideo being here is to give me feedback before I give this presentation to senior management, but I don't know how to interpret his comments. Does he or doesn't he like the presentation?"*

Hideo was direct; he didn't mince words, but it left Sandra stinging. The authenticity of his words were lost in the delivery. The feedback Sandra gathered was reinforced by Hideo's nonverbal behavior that included direct eye contact and a strong, commanding voice. Hideo considered his behavior direct, but Sandra felt it was blunt and cutting—obviously not his intended message. The term *"directness"* can be misleading. When used skillfully and in appropriate situations, direct feedback can be very effective.

Keep in mind the following tips regarding the level of directness when delivering feedback.

Know your audience—the person you're giving feedback to. Some people respond to high directness; others respond better when the feedback is softened, worded as a suggestion. The following two examples have the same content, but the level of directness can send very different messages.

"If a similar situation should happen again, you might want to contact the main office and see what resources are available."

"Next time ask for help."

(more direct approach)

(softened approach)

Feedback lets the sender know how the message is received. It also provides a message back to the sender. Hideo's feedback let Sandra know how her presentation was being received. The overall tone and directness also sent a strong message to her *(beyond the content of the presentation)*— a message she interpreted as questioning her credibility, and criticizing her performance.

Pay attention to nonverbal behavior. Words can reflect a softer approach, but the nonverbal behavior could be sending a conflicting message, one of directness.

Members of your diverse work group will have different preferences on directness. Your job is to determine what that level is so you can provide the best form of feedback.

Differences Of Formality

Another key element of communication and feedback in diverse work groups is differences in formality. That is, the amount of structure, form, and procedure for feedback.

What factors influence differences in formality in the feedback process?

♦ The maturity level of the group. New work-group members may need greater support and assurance that can be provided by structured, formal feedback.

♦ Specific work-group situations. Sometimes the leader (in taking cues from the work group) may decide to give a work group a more structured format on communication and feedback.

♦ Cultural background. Some cultures place a high value on formal communication and expect people to follow protocol and "rules" on feedback.

♦ The organization. The organization may have a culture which supports formal *(or informal)* feedback and communication.

♦ Be cautious about concluding too quickly about someone's preference for formality. You might be interpreting verbal and nonverbal clues through your own personal frame of reference and mistake the person's message. Knowing your audience and using the techniques of formality appropriately are the keys to effective feedback and communication.

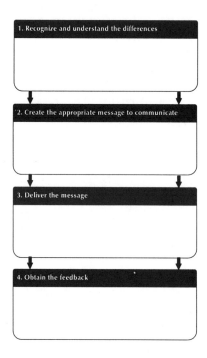

1. Recognize and understand the differences

2. Create the appropriate message to communicate

3. Deliver the message

4. Obtain the feedback

The Diversity Communication Planner is an excellent tool for constructing feedback. When factoring in the formality of differences, you'll want to carefully plan your communication for the most positive feedback experience.

Marv wanted his feedback...
to Olga to go well. He used the Diversity Communication Planner...

THE DIVERSITY COMMUNICATION PLANNER

1. Recognize and understand the differences

- I'll be giving formal performance feedback to Olga.

- Olga has a no-nonsense style. Her directness can be interpreted as abrupt and rude. I've worked with her long enough to know she is not making personal attacks. It's just her way of expressing herself.

- Olga is most comfortable when I provide a strong, authoritative position.

- She also prefers a high degree of formality regarding feedback.

2. Create the appropriate message to communicate

- Olga knows and has experienced formal performance feedback.

- Being straightforward with the performance feedback, is the message I need to deliver.

3. Deliver the message

- I'll conduct this feedback, just like the others, in the privacy of my office.

- The tone will be more formal.

- I'll take the lead in kicking-off the feedback discussion; however, I plan to ask questions to elicit her perspective. It will be valuable to see how she views her performance.

4. Obtain the feedback

- I know Olga well enough to read her nonverbal behavior. I'll make a note to pay attention to the nonverbals since she may not say much. This will let me know how she is responding to the feedback.

- I'll need to probe to determine if my feedback is coming across as I had intended. I plan to ask questions and to ask follow-up questions regarding her comments.

CHAPTER SEVEN WORKSHEET:
GIVING AND RECEIVING FEEDBACK
IN YOUR DIVERSE WORK GROUP

1. Think about your diverse work group. What format of feedback is best suited for your work group—traditional or multisource? Why?

_____

_____

_____

_____

2. If you are giving feedback, answer the following questions to help you plan your message and strategy.

   a. Who will be receiving your feedback?

_____

_____

   b. What do you know about this person's communication style and skills?

_____

_____

c. Does this person prefer high directness or low directness?

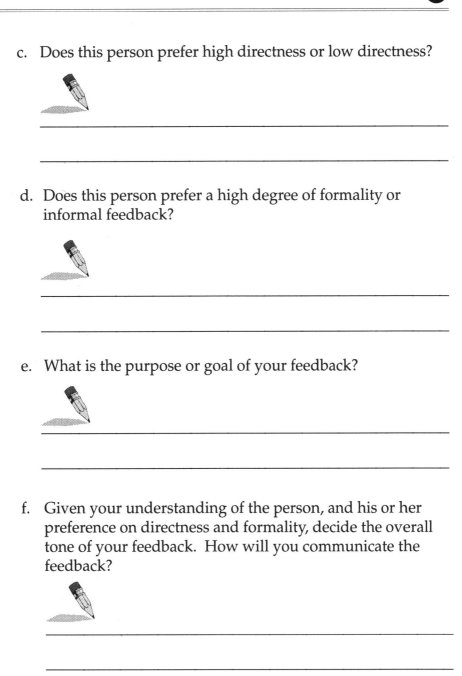

_____

_____

d. Does this person prefer a high degree of formality or informal feedback?

_____

_____

e. What is the purpose or goal of your feedback?

_____

_____

f. Given your understanding of the person, and his or her preference on directness and formality, decide the overall tone of your feedback. How will you communicate the feedback?

_____

_____

CHAPTER EIGHT

SUMMARY

Effective communication in a diverse work group requires conscious effort and skills. You may feel overwhelmed with all the elements and factors to consider. But you can successfully build your competence and skills in communicating in a diverse work group. Start out slowly and continue to explore new situations. You will find your confidence growing along with your ability to communicate in a variety of situations and settings.

Communication begins with a clear goal and purpose. What are you trying to get across? What do you hope to achieve? Remember, if you can't articulate the purpose of your communication, whether it's sending a message or giving feedback, hold off. Your ability to communicate with clarity begins when you are focused.

Also remember that what sets your work group apart from others is the diversity factor. Don't lose sight of the fundamental principle of diversity which is the acknowledgment and acceptance of differences in others. Communication is a powerful tool to maximize the talents of a diverse work group.

The term *"work group"* implies that people are drawn together for a common purpose or goal. Communication is the linkage that binds their thoughts, ideas, and vision. Successful communication can be a shared responsibility, with each work-group member accountable to each other.

Challenges and issues—such as work-group conflict, on-going motivation, and balancing talent—are in every group. These challenges are heightened in a diverse work group. As a leader, you may find yourself working harder on these issues, but they are manageable, and the rewards are tremendous.

REPRODUCIBLE FORMS AND WORKSHEETS

The pages in the Appendix are provided for you to photocopy and use appropriately.

THE DIVERSITY COMMUNICATION PLANNER

Name: _____ Date: _____

1. Recognize and understand the differences

2. Create the appropriate message to communicate

3. Deliver the message

4. Obtain the feedback

New Leader's
Communication Assessment Worksheet

Column I: Self-Assessment	Column II: Work Group	Column III: Comparison Between Column I and Column II	
		Areas where we agree	Areas where we differ
My preferred communication style when leading work groups: ♦ ♦ ♦ ♦ ♦ ♦ ♦	The preferred communication style of the work group given its diverse make-up: ♦ ♦ ♦ ♦ ♦ ♦ ♦		
To what extent am I open and accepting of differences in others? ♦ ♦ ♦ ♦ ♦ ♦ ♦	To what extent is the work group open and accepting of differences in each other? ♦ ♦ ♦ ♦ ♦ ♦		
To what extent am I committed to full utilization of the talents and skills of each work-group member? ♦ ♦ ♦ ♦ ♦ ♦ ♦	To what extent has the work group fully utilized the talents and skills of each work-group member? ♦ ♦ ♦ ♦ ♦ ♦		
My idea of successful communication in a diverse work group is: ♦ ♦ ♦ ♦ ♦ ♦	The group's idea of successful communication within a diverse work group is: ♦ ♦ ♦ ♦ ♦ ♦		

DIVERSITY COMMUNICATION STYLE CONTINUUM

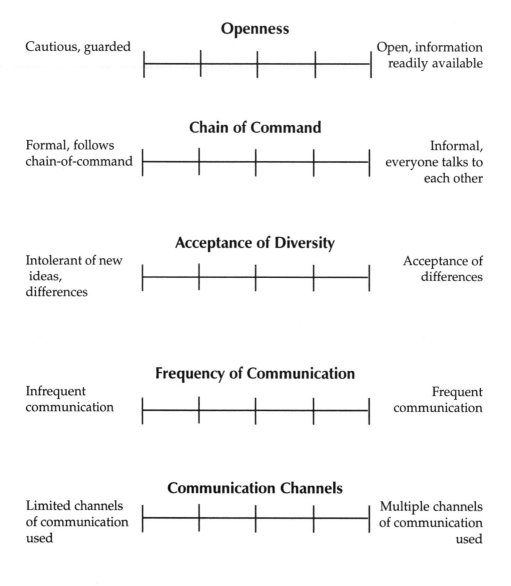

Openness

Cautious, guarded ├─────┼─────┼─────┼─────┤ Open, information readily available

Chain of Command

Formal, follows chain-of-command ├─────┼─────┼─────┼─────┤ Informal, everyone talks to each other

Acceptance of Diversity

Intolerant of new ideas, differences ├─────┼─────┼─────┼─────┤ Acceptance of differences

Frequency of Communication

Infrequent communication ├─────┼─────┼─────┼─────┤ Frequent communication

Communication Channels

Limited channels of communication used ├─────┼─────┼─────┼─────┤ Multiple channels of communication used

COMMUNICATION-PROBLEM ANALYSIS CHART

	Cause #1	Cause #2	Cause #3
	Why?	Why?	Why?
1.	because...	because...	because...
	Why?	Why?	Why?
2.	because...	because...	because...
	Why?	Why?	Why?
3.	because...	because...	because...
	Why?	Why?	Why?

CRITERIA RATING FORM

	Solution 1	Solution 2	Solution 3	Solution 4
Criterion A				
Criterion B				
Criterion C				
Criterion D				
Criterion E				
Criterion F				
Criterion G				
Total Score				

THE PRACTICAL GUIDEBOOK COLLECTION
FROM RICHARD CHANG ASSOCIATES, INC.
PUBLICATIONS DIVISION

Our Practical Guidebook Collection is growing to meet the challenges of the ever-changing workplace of the 90's. Available through Richard Chang Associates, Inc., fine bookstores, training and organizational development resource catalogs and distributed internationally.

QUALITY IMPROVEMENT SERIES

- Meetings That Work!
- Continuous Improvement Tools Volume 1
- Continuous Improvement Tools Volume 2
- Step-By-Step Problem Solving
- Satisfying Internal Customers First!
- Continuous Process Improvement
- Improving Through Benchmarking
- Succeeding As A Self-Managed Team
- Process Reengineering In Action
- Measuring Organizational Improvement Impact

MANAGEMENT SKILLS SERIES

- Coaching Through Effective Feedback
- Expanding Leadership Impact
- Mastering Change Management
- On-The-Job Orientation And Training
- Re-Creating Teams During Transitions

HIGH PERFORMANCE TEAM SERIES

- Success Through Teamwork
- Team Decision-Making Techniques
- Measuring Team Performance
- Building A Dynamic Team

HIGH-IMPACT TRAINING SERIES

- Creating High-Impact Training
- Identifying Targeted Training Needs
- Mapping A Winning Training Approach
- Producing High-Impact Learning Tools
- Applying Successful Training Techniques
- Measuring The Impact Of Training
- Make Your Training Results Last

WORKPLACE DIVERSITY SERIES

- Capitalizing On Workplace Diversity
- Successful Staffing In A Diverse Workplace
- Team Building For Diverse Work Groups
- Communicating In A Diverse Workplace
- Tools For Valuing Diversity

Additional Resources
From Richard Chang Associates, Inc.

Improve your training sessions and seminars with the ideal tools—videos from Richard Chang Associates, Inc. You and your team will easily relate to the portrayals of real-life workplace situations. You can apply our innovative techniques to your own situations for immediate results.

Training Videotapes

Mastering Change Management*
Turning Obstacles Into Opportunities

Step-By-Step Problem Solving*
A Practical Approach To Solving Problems On The Job

Quality: You Don't Have To Be Sick To Get Better**
Individuals Do Make a Difference

Achieving Results Through Quality Improvement**

*Authored by Dr. Richard Chang and produced by Double Vision Studios.
**Produced by American Media Inc. in conjunction with Richard Chang Associates, Inc.
  Each video includes a Facilitator's Guide.

"The Human Edge Series" Videotapes

Total Quality: Myths, Methods, Or Miracles
Featuring Drs. Ken Blanchard and Richard Chang

Empowering The Quality Effort
Featuring Drs. Ken Blanchard and Richard Chang

Produced by Double Vision Studios.

"The Total Quality Series"
Training Videotapes And Workbooks

Building Commitment *(Telly Award Winner)*
How To Build Greater Commitment To Your TQ Efforts

Teaming Up
How To Successfully Participate On Quality-Improvement Teams

Applied Problem Solving
How To Solve Problems As An Individual Or On A Team

Self-Directed Evaluation
How To Establish Feedback Methods To Self-Monitor Improvements

Authored by Dr. Richard Chang and produced by Double Vision Studios, each videotape from *"The Total Quality Series"* includes a *Facilitator's Guide* and five *Participant Workbooks* with each purchase. Additional *Participant Workbooks* are available for purchase.

EVALUATION AND FEEDBACK FORM

We need your help to continuously improve the quality of the resources provided through the Richard Chang Associates, Inc., Publications Division. We would greatly appreciate your input and suggestions regarding this particular guidebook, as well as future guidebook interests.

Please photocopy this form before completing it, since other readers may use this guidebook. Thank you in advance for your feedback.

Guidebook Title: _____

1. Overall, how would you rate your *level of satisfaction* with this guidebook? Please circle your response.

   Extremely Dissatisfied   Satisfied   Extremely Satisfied

        1   2   3   4   5

2. What specific *concepts or methods* did you find <u>most</u> helpful?

   _____

   _____

3. What specific *concepts or methods* did you find <u>least</u> helpful?

   _____

   _____

4. As an individual who may purchase additional guidebooks in the future, what *characteristics/features/benefits* are most important to you in making a decision to purchase a guidebook *(or another similar book)*?

   _____

   _____

5. What additional *subject matter/topic areas* would you like to see addressed in future guidebooks?

   _____

   _____

Name *(optional)*:_____

Address: _____

C/S/Z: _____   **Phone (   )** _____

PLEASE FAX YOUR RESPONSES TO: (714) 756-0853
OR CALL US AT: 1-800-756-8096